HOMELESS, In My Own Words:

True stories of homeless mothers

BY GAIL LUKASIK

First Edition

Cover Photography and design: Gail Lukasik

"Deborah" first appeared in *The Illinois Review*.

Homeless, In My Own Words was performed at Barat College and The Art Institute of Chicago.

Dedicated to homeless mothers, their children, and homeless shelters

PREFACE

Homeless, In My Own Words has been a long time in the making. I began this book project in 1989 and spent about a year interviewing 14 homeless women with children living in Chicago area shelters. My plan was to work collaboratively with a photographer on a book that explored the experiences of homeless mothers through photographs and text.

What I was seeking were the stories behind the statistics. I knew that women with children were the fastest growing segment of the homeless. Today families are the fastest growing segment of the homeless. I also knew that these women and their children were called the invisible homeless, because you don't see them on the streets. I discovered that the cause of their homelessness was a complex series of events that spanned their lifetimes. But more importantly, I discovered who these women were.

My original idea was to write short journalistic pieces about the women accompanied by their photographs. When the collaboration with the photographer didn't work out, I was left with hours and hours of taped interviews and no photographs. For several years, I struggled with the form the material would take.

While doing an artist residency at Ragdale Foundation, I began to see that the strength of these women's stories was their words. And that only the poetic monologue captured each woman's individual voice and story. Through poetry I could emphasize both the story and the conversational style of each woman. In that way these rich but harrowing stories could be fully comprehended and appreciated as instructive as well as cautionary tales.

All the stories are true. The words are the women's words—edited and put into poetic form. Their stories are graphic, honest, and painful. Although these women are rejects of society, oppressed and depressed, they shine in the power of their voices. They are angry, but they do not view themselves as lost. They may talk about being victims, but it's less to gain your pity than to mesmerize you. And isn't that what good storytellers do. These strange women, these revealers, these storytellers will show you the unknown, the unseen, and the unheard.

How these stories changed my own life is for another book. I don't pretend to understand what it's like to be without a physical place to live. I have never been homeless in that way. But as the daughter of a mother who grew up being passed from home to home, I inherited my mother's sense of homelessness. Linda, one of the homeless mothers, best describes the homelessness I share with these women: "It's like I've been in a homeless state of mind all my life."

DuPage Emergency Shelter
DuPage, IL
Joanne (37): *I'll tell you what it's like*
                    Children: Sarah 16, Tim 15, Thomas 8

There are empty boxes and minimal furniture in the two-bedroom basement apartment. Joanne and her three children sleep on box springs without mattresses. It's been four days since they've left the DuPage Emergency Shelter, where they spent the last three weeks.

It's a rainy November night. I've been working on the project for eight months. And it's beginning to wear on me. Each interview takes from three to four hours. I listen to their stories, sitting on bunk beds, at kitchen tables, in hallways, and in dirt yards. Each story is a testament to a life gone astray.

JOANNE

I.
I'll tell you what it's like.
It's not like you can't have Reeboks
or a pair of Nikes.
It means you can't have shoes.
You have to wear the same shoes
with the holes in them every day.

It's not like you can't have steak for dinner
or you can't have lettuce.
It's that there's no food in the cabinets
or in the refrigerator,
there's no money to get it
and God please provide us food
for the day.

Or we've eaten beans and rice
or we've eaten macaroni until
it's come out of our ears and potatoes.
Whatever it takes to make it to the next day.

And my kids have gone through a lot.
They say, you know, your kids have to toughen
up. My kids are plenty tough.

So when people say you don't understand,
I understand a lot.
I understand a lot more than I want.

II.
First my family said,
"What we'll do, cause we're really upset
that you're in a shelter home,
we'll come and take your kids."
That was their first,
that was their decision
that they're going to do.
A bunch of them got together
to tell me this. It was like in the pit
of my stomach. I just knew
I wanted to puke all over the place.

So it's all the time and
then their father blows in
periodically and says,
"You know, you're an unfit mother.
You are not doing the best you can."
"Here take this boy," I told him.
"Here, take this boy to your home."

But he doesn't take the kids.
He didn't want them,
doesn't pay for them.
But I was unfit,
I took this and absorbed it.
When he calls me unfit,
I find it very hard
to swallow at times.

III.
So I called my mother,
"Mother, I'm being evicted from my house down here.
Can we come and stay?"
"Call me back in a couple of weeks, I'll think about it."

So when we came here I called my mother again.
"Mother, you know about coming."
And she said, "All right." Finally, she agreed. She said, "2 months."

It was Thursday.
We'd only been there since Saturday.
It was 10:30 at night.
And I thought I didn't hear anything.
I went downstairs.
It was my mistake.
She was sitting at the table waiting.
Waiting for me.
And she sat there and told me
that I was a grotesque animal
that needed to be in a zoo with a keeper.
That I was repugnant to her.
That she wouldn't even touch
my slimly self-
centered self-
righteous
viperous
bitch body.
So that night I stayed up and waited.

IV.
There's ten of us.
We all take the abuse.
It used to be physical
now it's verbal.
What we're talking about is leather straps,
the whole 9 yards. My mother used to
chain us to things.
What we would do
on weekends, on Saturdays, we would
have what we call the lineup.
And all of us
who were old enough to stand
in the hallway, she would find
something that happened during the week
and one of us
would have to take a beating for it.
And so during the week we would decide
whose turn it was. And it was
the 4 oldest ones.
And we would decide who
would take the beating.
So that the youngest ones
wouldn't have to.

V.
And you think it would be easy enough
to take a handful of pills, you know.
It was terrible. I was riding down
the streets of Kentucky.
It was terrible.
And my son was at this carnival
and it was late at night
and I was tired
and it was almost before we were going to be evicted
and I knew we were coming to Chicago
and I was crying
and I was really upset
and it was like 2 o'clock in the morning
I was just driving
and in Kentucky there's no such thing
as a straight road
everything is
you know
winding and curvy
and I was driving on the road
and I said, "Oh God, I'm just going to go home
and take a handful of pills,
I'm just going to take these things
and get it over with." I said, "The kids
have got insurance. They'll be fine."
I said, "Why not just go on
and kill me."
And out of the corner of my eye
I saw the biggest blackest dog
I have ever seen in my life. He came
trotting right in front of my car. So,
of course, I had to veer out of the way
not to hurt this dog. First, I'm crying
and then I'm hysterically laughing.
I thought, God that's not exactly what I meant
by dying. I meant I want something
where I have a smile on my face
when I die. Not with this dog,
You know. With a dog of all things.
I hate dogs.

VI.
I don't have the luxury of a little
nervous breakdown or a little
time out. I have to keep pressing
forwards at what I'm doing
if I'm going to make it
to the end of this.
I need to keep running
the race. I can't spend time
you know
copping out and
looking for ways to

So it means don't get sick,
don't need a break
nothin' just continue
until you drop.

SARAH (Joanne's daughter)

I.
Most of the time we really wanted to get out
of those places. Those were bad neighborhoods.
Besides we would have to get out sooner or later.
And none of my friends knew
we got evicted. They just knew
we moved out. Mom said,
"Oh, we're going to live in the car."
It scared me but you know,
we're not that kind of people.

Mom slept in the car and Tom, all he did was cry.
"I don't want to sleep in a car."
I stayed at my friend's house.
So I had a place, but not my mom.
So she had to sleep in the car and
all Tom did was cry the whole time.
"I don't want to sleep in the car."
And I never seen him cry like that before.

II.
When my ma came to pick me up from school,
she said, "We're going to the shelter."
I thought, "Oh my gosh, a shelter."
I thought, "There's all these bums there."
And I said, "I don't want to go."
I said, "I'm not going."

Because most homeless people are bums and alcoholics and stuff,
Not people. And I just didn't want to say to my best friend,
"Oh, I'm living in a shelter home."
I was afraid of how she would look at me.

III.
So I said, "I'm not staying there."
And mom said, "You can stay with you grandma."

I could have gone with my aunts or my grandma,
But I stayed with my mom and brothers.
Because you just don't desert your family
when they're that down in the dumps.

IV.
So when we first got there, I said, "Oh, this is weird."
I didn't know what to expect.
But we went back to our room and
it was really nice and
the people there weren't bums.
They were real nice to you.
So it was a lot different than I thought it would be.
It was like a hotel, really.
And I met a lot of people in the shelter.
I did make a lot of new friends.
I just didn't think it would be like that.
After I was there a few days, it wasn't that bad.

V.
I know a couple of times I got mad at her
and brought it up that we're living here.
She said, "I really feel bad enough,
we have to be here."

I felt bad afterwards.
But she knew I was sorry, but . . .

VI.
I was at Eisenhower 3 days.
I was at Willowbrook 5 days.
Now I'm at Addison.
I changed schools 3 times this year.
It's really not that hard
meeting new people.

But moving around like today
I didn't want to get up and go to another school.
It's stupid.
They're going to get sick of me moving.
I don't want to flunk.

But it's not really bad,
moving to all these different schools.
Because it's been easier to meet friends
than I thought it would be.
It's really not that hard
meeting new friends.

VII.
It's not what I expected.
It's not really as bad as you'd expect it to be
I mean; Yeah, my mom didn't have a job
And you don't have a place but it's, I mean,
you feel bad, you have low esteem and all that--
I'm in this terrible place and all that.
But you have to look on the bright side
that you're not the only person that's like this.

So you can't really feel all that bad
and think you're the only person and
feel ashamed and all that--
but you know there are thousands of people out there.
And it's not really what I expected.
It's not really so bad as you'd expect,
I mean . . .
It's really not so hard,
it's not really so bad . . .

Housing Opportunities for Women (HOW)
Rogers Park, IL
Linda (34): *I've been in a homeless state of mind all my life*
One Child: Cynthia 13

Linda is big-boned and blonde with short-cropped hair. She's living temporarily in a HOW apartment that she shares with two other women. She has her own bedroom and has been clean of drugs and alcohol for three months. On her bed are stuffed animals. Next to her bed is a picture of her daughter, Cynthia.

She breaks down only once during the interview; when she talks about letting her sister-in-law legally adopt her daughter, because she was too drugged up to care for her. We're sitting at the kitchen table; I reach my hand out to offer her comfort. She pulls away.

I'm beginning to feel the strain of listening to so much pain.

LINDA

I.

I got pregnant and I had to have an abortion. He didn't want any more children. He had four from his wife. I didn't know if I wanted to have the child. I don't think I did. I hated him for wanting me to have the abortion. I felt that was wrong. I don't think deep inside, I wanted the child either.

II.
His ex-wife and I tried to do a home job. You know, with the coat hanger and drinking the castor oil. But nothing happened.
She said, "You're a real strong-bodied kid."
I guess so.

She used a coat hanger and a urethra tube. You try to break through the uterus to bust the bag. But it wouldn't work.
Not just that she was afraid of hurting me. She knew what she was doing, but she never performed it on anybody else. She done it to herself. And it worked. So she thought it would work for me, but it wouldn't.

III.
Tom used to beat me a lot, so if I didn't do this I was afraid I'd get my ass whooped. So I'd better do it. Just slap me around. I'll do it. Eventually I had the abortion in Chicago. That was before I left, before he pulled the shotgun on me. When I saw the gun, I said, "That's it."

IV.
I think he whooped me the worse than any of them did. He would go nuts. I was like always having a black eye. Always.
He's much bigger than I was. He would come home and I'd be asleep and he's thinking I was passed out from drinkin' and druggin'. We'd get into a fight and you know he started hitting me and I started hitting him.

And it just went around like that. It was--yeah I know I fucked up and if this is your way of dealing with me. Knock your socks off.
To me, I always said to myself, he'll be the loser in the long run, because I'll just leave. I'm not going to deal with this.
But I don't leave right away. It's like I have to get a real good ass whipping.

One day he kicked me with his steel-toed boots. He kicked me in the face. That was the breaking point. I lay there and couldn't move and was like I thought every bone in my body was broke. It was like--you know Linda the secret to this is you either change your life or stay this way and die. I left.

V.

I guess that's really when I became homeless. I met this guy. We lived in the streets. We lived in abandoned buildings. We went to churches for food. We went to Salvation Army at 2 or 1 everyday to eat lunch. We were really lucky.

We had this one abandoned building where we wired up electricity. We had a heater-type thing in one of the bedrooms with a mattress on the floor. Two little milk cartons with a piece of a table. Hot plate on that. Pulled in a chair from outside, pulled in a television from outside that worked from the alley. We had running water. We were the only people in there. It was a nice house.

Lots of nights we slept on the streets. We didn't find this place right away. This wasn't a right away thing.

We slept in hallways of buildings. Lot of times I'd go to an open car. Lot of times I wasn't with him. Sometimes I'd take off, because I could do better by myself. By that time I wasn't scared someone would attack me. By that time, me and 63rd street, I knew 63rd street like the back of my hand. Knew everybody on it, and everybody knew me as long as I was on 63rd street, between Western and California.

It's where you get real secure with that. There was this one guy at the Laundromat, Bill; he would let me stay at the Laundromat. I could wash my clothes and take a shower. I did that for 5 years, on and off, living that way.

VI.

Again, I'm out here.

It was like, I was always too out of it, for it not to be okay to live like this.

It's like, I've never really had what you call a home. Like I could say this is my house or this is where I live. It's like I've been in a homeless state of mind all my life.

My father's was a physical abuse, which the bruises went away. My mother's was a mental, which I'm still trying to work through those. She raised me with: you're no good. I was bitches and whores before I knew what sex was. She would just have a frenzy. I was all kinds of bitches and whores and I didn't know what they were.

I think I was 12 or 13, I went and dyed my hair and shaved off my eyebrows and I said: "This is what whores really look like, isn't it?"

She made me go to school that way, she did. I wanted to die. My hair turned orange and I didn't know how to use the pencil on my eyebrows. She made me go to school that way.

My mother abandoned me. My dad is always with me. It's a strange kind of bondage.

I remember being 32 years old and sitting on a bench with a bottle of Jubilee wine in my hand just looking at everybody. It was winter. I guess that's why I get so depressed in winter. It's cold out and here I am sitting here, a mess and don't give a shit. It made no sense to me.

St. Francis de Paula Shelter, Catholic Charities
Chicago, IL
Margaret (45): *I was bad*
Five children: Anthony 26, Trina 19, Arinza 15, Sonia 14, Orin 4

There are deep scars running parallel up and down the insides of Margaret's arms. She shows me them as proof of a love she once had for her husband and a reminder that no one can treat her that way anymore.

In the 8 x 8 third floor room at St. Francis de Paula shelter, Margaret, her 4-year-old son, Orion, and 14-year-old daughter, Sonia have crammed all their belongings. There are clothes scattered on the bed, on the floor, in the tiny closet.

No one is smiling.

MARGARET

I.
I was bad
I know I was
bad the state said so
the state said that if momma didn't
sign the papers they would cut
off the welfare
my momma was ignorant
to the fact that they couldn't
do that but it worked
she took me out there
to Dickson mental
I was 7
then stayed 11
years when I left
there I was 18
I was real resentful to that
at the time I was ignorant to
the fact that they couldn't
do that

II.
I've had a hell of a life.
But I've come up
roses. Because in that hospital
if I weren't
as strong as I
am, as smart as I am,
I be a vegetable.
Because I had to take care
of babies and crazy people.
They had some nuts
out there. I was working
when I was 9 or 10
in the laundry,
in the bakery,
in the nursery.
When I get crazy,
they shoot me
full of that Thorazine and
choke me
till I pass out. But
they shot me full
of that Thorazine and then I be
walking around like a zombie
for a couple of days. I'm not
stupid. They give me
those shock treatments
too. Put me in
that tub. Cold
water. If I wasn't strong
up here. I'd be gone
a long time ago. But
I was bad.
It felt horrible.
Like somebody poked you
with a bunch of icicles
all at one time.
I took care of the state
for a long time.
they can take care
of me for a little while.

III.
I was bad
terrible I wasn't home
a month 'fore I was
pregnant I never been
with nobody.
I got a son 26
a daughter 19
another son 15
another daughter 14
and a son 4
I've been on
welfare ever since
I had that baby and I'm 45
I don't like it
I've had jobs I was a
nurse's aid, switchboard
operator and a
waitress, short
order cook and a
whore for a
long time I was
bad I got married
too once I used to do
heroin years ago
10 years I was on
the streets working, I was
a lady
of the evening to keep up
with my habit because
I was taking care
of my husband's habit
too

IV.
And I had a house then.
When I was on the streets.
I had a place
to stay. I was doing everything
against the law, but I had
a place to stay
and ate good every day.
I was living good.
Ate anything I wanted.
I didn't have to wait
for nobody
to give it to me.

V.
They say I'm bad.
They say I'm threading
on thin ice and if I do anything
by Friday, they'll kick me out.
When they kick me out,
there's no other shelter
going to take me.
They keep that in your face
all the time. This is a good place,
but they keep that in your face,
that they'll throw you out.

VI.
The only reason that I'm here
is that some days I be so
depressed that I smoke up
all my money. I'll smoke up
every damn dime.
I did coke, too. But
it ain't done me no good.
I won't tell no lie.
I drink me some beer and some wine.
I ain't doing drugs,
because if I was
I would say I was.

My kids
that's all
I live for,
that's all
I got.
Everything else
is gone. If it don't be
for my kids,
then forget it.
Every day my little girl comes in,
she say, "Are we getting put out?"
Because I must have a look
sometimes on my face
after they holler at me
or I done something wrong.
Everybody can tell
when I'm sad.
My little boy knows.
I just lay on that floor
and my little boy says to me,
"Mommy, are you mad at me?
Are you sad today?"

VII.
Sometimes I be depressed,
because I'm tired of this.
They keep telling me
that they're going to give me
a place and everyone that I go to
they send me to someone else.
They say a couple of months.
It's been a couple of months.
This is an emergency.
I'm about to go
crazy and so is my kids.

The state ain't going to do nothin',
I don't put no emphasis on it,
because I know
they ain't going to do nothin',
but what they're doing right now:
sending me a check and food stamps.

I could tell you a lot of things
they should do for me.
All the years they taken away from me.
I think there's a lot of things
they should do for me.
Why should I even go into it,
because they ain't going to do it?
When I think about it--
I've been institutionalized
all my life. From one end to another--
that's the truth. From 7 until I'm 45.

I consider this an institution
for the homeless. You can give me
money and food stamps,
what am I going do with it?
Besides smoke it up
or shoot it up
or drink it up,
if I'm not in here.

VIII.
My kids it's all
I got. My little boy
he's only 4 but
you think he was 7.
I make it a point to let him know
that this is not our real house.
We're just here for a visit.
This is a shelter:
St. Francis de Paula.
He knows exactly where he's at.
Everywhere he goes he knows.
He can tell you where he's at.
Cause you say to him,
"Where you live Orin?"
And he says,
"The shelter home,"
Big as day.
They know.

Assumption, BVM Shelter Home, Catholic Charities
Chicago, IL
Deborah (31): *I didn't even know where I was sometime*
Four children: Denee 14, Renee 11, Debra 10, Eddy 7

We sit on lawn chairs in a long, narrow room at the back of the shelter home. The door is closed and it's late morning. A yellow warm light makes everything seem too close. Deborah drifts in and out of reality; at least that's what I tell myself. Not because I don't believe her, but because I do. She is strikingly pretty. But there is a certain inattention in her eyes that scares me.

DEBORAH

I.

Sixty-third and Cottage Grove, South Parkway—I couldn't tell you
the other places.
Until I was about seven, in various different places, on the south
side mostly, I lived.

II.
One morning I got up and they said they had taken my mother
during the night.
Two ladies came and said we were going to a foster home.
We were split up two and two.

My younger sister was beaten a lot.
My baby brother was adopted out.

I don't know why we were taken from my mother. All I know is
that they gave us to the wrong people.

III.
It's horrible to never have a permanent place.
I didn't even know where I was sometime.
I woke up in school. I didn't know what school I was in.
It was different.
I got lost until six or seven that evening. I didn't know my
way home. I was too scared to ask anyone,
because I didn't even know where I was asking to go.

IV.
There was a time my father went after my mother with a butcher knife.
There was a time my mother had 80 stitches on her leg.

My mother died when I was 12. I'm told she died of suicide
but I'm not sure. There were several stories--

Some said she was pushed out the window,
some said she jumped.

My father got custody.
My father got us.

V.
From my father, from my mother's brother, from this minister
who was taking care of us when my mother was working as a waitress
and from the guys who broke into our apartment, tied up my mother,
and raped her.
I saw this, but one boy bothered with me as well.
I'm not clear what happened to my mother
and why these people came.

VI.
I mean it was like my father had things sort of in his pocket.
I mean one time he knocked me down to the ground on Grace and
Broadway. I'll never forget it:
I was 15, I had come home from swimming,
he kept telling me that I'd better tell him I was high.
I said no,
and he knocked me down to the ground,
and I saw a squad car go by
when I was getting up from the ground,
no one did anything—I'll never forget it.

VII.
One time I was real upset, I was tired of the stuff that was
going on at home.
And my girl friends, they were doing drugs and stuff like that,
and they decided that they were going to go and buy Richard's--
everybody pitched in--so I decided to,
so we chipped in and bought two bottles of Richard's Wild
Irish Rose and we drank it,
and I started getting drunk and they started smoking reefer
and I took two puffs of it and then I went home.

And when I went home my father was the only one there,
and I'm like, okay now you really got a reason to beat me up.
And he says hi. And I says, hello—
and I knew he had to smell it—
and he just walked away and went into his room.
And that let me know then that he didn't want good for me.

VIII.
When you're constantly living like a prisoner, you know,
you snap.
One time I wrote my father a letter saying I was going to get
out of here,
even if it took me to get pregnant. He started smacking me,
slamming me against the wall.
Things happen: I became pregnant—I didn't tell anyone—
I didn't panic.
I felt, well, then my father would throw me out,
but it didn't work that way.
We still have to stay there. We still have to stay there
and then it was real hard.

IX.
So then I went to live with the father of the baby. He didn't
believe in birth control,
and he also believed in having children as a punishment towards
me,
so he would hide or burn up my birth control.

When he decided that it was time for me to become pregnant,
he would take his kids to his mother's house,
and we would be there for a few days, until he figured that
was enough,
and I would get pregnant.

X.
I married him because he agreed then that he would leave me
alone.
It was the only reason. I mean he dragged me down the street,
and I mean nobody did nothing.

It was the same thing as he dragged me to his house—all the people
out there—no one ever called the police. Same thing when he
dragged me to the board of health clinic to get the blood tests.

He was just a mean person, very much, he abused me. His mother
knew.
Nobody would say anything, because that was her son.
I'm sure she heard, I'm sure she saw the bruises.

I mean he was meeting me on the El trains. People would be there
and listen to this stuff and no one ever went to get the conductor
or anything, nothing.
People sit there and watch and they do nothing.

You know, there's not much you can do when you go to court,
and it's your word against another person's word,
and no one else will come up and speak up and be a witness.

XI.
First I used to keep myself together for my sisters, then it
was for my kids,
then it was like two years ago, it was like I felt I couldn't
keep together for anyone.

And I knew two years ago, I knew that if I took much more
of this—
if I had to be beat a few more times—
either I was going to be hospitalized or more
I felt fear really setting in me, very deeply,
and I said, "I can't do this anymore."

XII.
This was the youngest boy's father beating me then: he was like
right there when I was about to be rid of the girl's father.
It was like, it was like, I can get away, but there was another
one just waiting there.
It was like, I don't know, it was like a plan or something.
I couldn't be totally dependent on myself.

Every time I went to school either I became pregnant or
I got beaten so bad I had to stay home or whatever.

XIII.
He could come in and see one fork in the dish drainer
and decide we have to have—he always called it—a discussion.

I did try to fight back, all the time, but when you fight back
they beat you more,
and they enjoy what they're doing more.
They're very, he was very sadistic with sex, you know, fighting
back just really thrilled him.

XIV.

Cause it was like right near the end, they knew that I was
somehow going to get away,
and that's when the violence would become even the greatest,
and that's when they started in on the kids.

Like with my ex-husbands, like when my youngest daughter was
about two months—not long after she was born—
and then he had raised my daughter up in the air and let her fall
to the ground.
And see, I had caesarean, and he knew I was at my weakest point,
and he had not long after taken me and thrown me against the wall, some of the stitches
busted open and I had to go to the emergency
room. He was upset, because that was like:
"Did you tell anybody?"
I didn't and I kept telling him I didn't but he didn't believe it.
So then he took it out on my daughter. That was his kid.
It was like, they don't care.

Same thing with the little boy's dad. He beat his son the second,
the third day after he was hit by a car.
He had a broken leg, his whole forehead was swollen,
and he takes and starts with the belt buckle.
It was like, I saw it, but yet, I couldn't jump and run right
away to stop him.
You know, I think he had been hitting him with this thick leather
strap, with this big metal thing, like a good three, four minutes,
before I was able to get there to stop him.
He was only two.

XV.
And when I says that, he took his fist and hit me in the head.
I felt like I was ready to pass out, so I pretended to.
Because I knew if I got up, he was just going to hit me again.
Cause I knew that's all he wanted to do.

And then I got up, then I went to get ice for my head, because
I been pretending to pass out for 15 minutes.

You know what, I knew then that this guy would just let me die.
I could see now, I saw that my life was not going to be too much
longer after that.
You know, like this has got to end.

XVI.
I tremble, I cry, I sound like a loud cry, I feel it. Sometimes
I can be awake, and I can see that violence that happened long ago.
Sometimes it's the violence that the fathers' kids have done,
other times when I was younger, when I was with my mother,
or I was with my father, stepmother's brother, that kind of stuff.

I didn't talk about my flashbacks. You know, I told them
I couldn't sleep.

XVII.
My father used to make this prophesy to me, you know, I was
this soul-tainted child that was now a soul-tainted woman,
that he would be sure that my life would be just as miserable.

All he ever did was took away my dreams.

Sister Connie Driscoe*
St. Martin de Pores House of Hope

"You have to tell the truth about the homeless," Sister Connie says to me. She is the force behind St. Martin de Pores women's shelter, which is sandwiched between Hyde Park and the ghetto. She accepts no money from the Archdiocese of Chicago to run the shelter because of the birth control issue. Nor does she accept any money from the city.

"Anything the city gets involved in, it's a mess," says Driscoe. "All our funding comes from private donations."

Sister Connie wears an eye patch, drinks Scotch-whiskey, and is rumored to keep a gun. I saw the whiskey, but I can't vouch for the gun. But if the barbwire that surrounds the shelter's backyard is any indication of Sr. Connie's idea of security, I believe the gun rumor.

I ask Sister Therese about the barbwire fence and she tells me that after a father stole one of his children from the yard, they put up the barbwire. I wonder if it goes both ways—meant to keep in as well as keep out.

* Sister Connie Driscoe died in 2005.

St. Martin de Porres House of Hope
Chicago, IL
Cammie (29): *It's something that never / leaves a person*
One child: Cammie three weeks

Cammie is thin, swaybacked, and college educated. She's escaped giving birth on the street by four days. There are two, low windows and a small desk in the entranceway where we sit. She never cries. Her voice, steady and quiet, is weighted with a resignation I have yet to understand.

A year later, when I call the shelter to follow up on some of the women, I learn that Cammie has managed to turn her life around. No longer homeless, she has a job and is raising her daughter. And she has just been diagnosed with terminal cancer.

CAMMIE

I.
When I went
to him and told
him I was pregnant
he denied the baby.
In some manner
I think he wanted me
to have an abortion
with her. I didn't want
to kill my baby at all.
He gave me a choice:
"Either you get rid of her
or hit the road,"
was his exact
words. And I hit
the road.

II.
He's much
older than me.
He's enough
for my father.
He accused me
of sleeping around.
I don't even like sex.
"C'mon with me," he said.
"I'll look out for you,"
And I was
28 at the time.
That's the whole thing
his being an older man.
I dare not move in
with anybody
my own age.
Then I have to deal
with the garbage,
his wanting to have
sex every night.

His age got me
where I was.
He's 59.
You know the old saying:
When a young woman date
an older man it's because of what
she didn't get from her father.

III.
See, I don't think
I'd ever
100% trust
a man. When I
sleep, I pretty much
sleep with one eye
open. I think about
85% is all
you're going to get
from me and I think
you're doing great there.

That's what I
meant about not liking
sex. It took all my
strength just to let
that old man touch
me. And
he knew that.
Why would he think
I'd have sex
with anyone else?

IV.
I didn't want
to kill this baby.
Because I didn't expect
I'll have another.
Seeing how I feel
about men. And
he said, "The last woman who told
me she was pregnant by me
accidentally fell
down the stairs
and had a miscarriage."
I got my stuff
And left. I actually think
this man would have
tried to kill me.

He was good
to me until I got
pregnant. He
changed because I would not
kill my baby.
But this is my
child. He say,
"I didn't father no baby.
You're out there
with younger men.
You're out there
screwing around."

V.
I never wanted to
get married because
of the marriage I
witnessed as a child. I
was always petrified. I
was so terrified of my
father that when he'd
stick the key through
the door, I'd just
run and find
the nearest hiding
place. Because that meant
danger. That was bad news.

VI.
We were all
too afraid to tell
because he would
threaten us and
there was no need
to disbelieve him.
Because he said he would
kill you,
he would do it.

I have seen him
pull knives
on my mother. He
almost have killed
her. He always
have a knife
or a blunt
object in his
hand. Never a fist.
I was afraid
to tell
her. I was
4 or 5
at the time. If
I was to tell
her that my father was
molesting
me and she'd
approach him,
my mother
would probably
die. He probably
would kill her.

I was protecting
her,
to protect
us.

VII.
As time went
on, I found
out he was
doing it to my
other sisters. That didn't
come out until after
I started not able
to hold my urine.

I went to
the doctor's. He said,
"Someone was messing
with your daughter." But
he didn't come right out
because again
like I say
it was the 60s.
I do recall
him saying, "Well, who
you leaving her with?"
It still
lingers today.
It's something that never
leaves a person. I
think it went till
7. It went
on for a long
time.
He used
his mouth on
me and that
I'll never
forget.

Because
my sisters, he
used to penetrate
them. Because their
hymen was broken.
That was
for sure. He never
penetrated me. But this
was something I don't care
how old
you always
remember.

You know
he used his mouth
on me. Stuff like
that. You don't
forget. As a child
I remember
myself
what went
on.

St. Martin de Porres House of Hope
Chicago, IL
Rosalind (28): *Yeah, I'm sleeping in a car / with my kids*
Three children: April 7, Chantevie, 6, Nicole, 4.

Rosalind is beautiful, her lovely face framed by a patterned turban that covers her hair.
She gazes at me with a pleading innocence. She has a halting way of speaking as if she
doesn't believe in her own words. Though her husband has abandoned her and her
children, it's clear she would go back to him in a heartbeat.

ROSALIND

I.
So I hate him, my husband.
I'm not sure
what he did. They said,
he took something,
you know from the government. He says he didn't.
They say, there could be something
else. I'm not sure, I know
only what he told me. At the time
I was, my baby was in the hospital.
She has asthma. And he comes
and brings this to me.
The only thing I could feel
was hatred for him.
For lack of, he just didn't
show any kind of
consideration for what was going on.
So, you know, I mean, like
up until this day
I think, I really, I just
hate him. There's no way,
you know, to put it.
I just hate him.

II.
I came back
for them. I came back
to Chicago, to my sister's.
She's married.
She has an apartment.
She has 6 kids,
I have 3.

Like her husband told us,
he says, "It was just the women
that had the problem." He says,
"Women can't live together."
He says that.

III.
My husband had decided that he was,
that he couldn't take it
anymore. So he went
with a brother. And me and
the kids slept in a car.
Yeah, I'm sleeping in a car
with my kids. We did it
in a drive-in, in a driveway.
Yeah, it was safe. Well, it was
not a cold day, it was a
rainy night. But it was not
cold. Then my, my,
my daughter got sick.
We were closed
inside the car, it was raining
that night. It wasn't really
that cold.

Yeah, my sister-in-law,
her husband, her two kids, my three kids,
and me. Yeah, in one car.

So yeah, it was really,
it was a compact car,
a small car, but
we managed. It was like
I had my oldest
across me, then she
across her, then my other
on her. It wasn't the most
comfortable but at least
we weren't out in the streets.

IV.
I was scared, you know,
I stayed woke mostly
all night, I was afraid
then my daughter got sick,
then she started to hyperventilate
because they had the heat on
and the windows up. Then her asthma came on
and she got really sick.

We did it for two days.
That was all,
that was about all
any of us could take.
And the only reason why
we had to do it then
because it was a weekend
and DHS said that
they didn't have anywhere.
But by the night
I had just about had it.
I had just about had it with DHS,
my husband, with you know, he's not around
and there was nobody but me and my kids
and the only alternative
was to sleep in the car.

V.
So we didn't, we hadn't had
a lot to eat. We went out
got like some rice.
Basically I wasn't, they were
eating. I wasn't. I wanted
to have enough for them
to keep going around
as much as I could
keep it. It was like
about two days. It was like
I was drinking water
to keep my stomach full.

VI.
I was frightened
of the reality
I'm all alone just me and the kids.
I don't have any money.
If, um,
if I,
if, um
at the moment, you know,
then if I wouldn't have, um
if I didn't know, um,
there was another alternative,
I would have just
killed us all,
because, um,
like I said
we hadn't been eating.
We were ready
for shelter.

VII.
If I did go back
it would be for them
not for me. Not at all,
for me. Because of all
the hurt that I think he put,
he put our lives in
not caring what he did
to us or, or the prices
we had to pay.
I mean, I don't see a real,
something real. Maybe something
to help me
get by with them.
But that's it.
I don't think
I ever want
him again.

VIII.
Yeah, I felt, you know,
maybe everyone's thinking
it's my fault. I'm not
taking care of things.
I shouldn't have had the kids.
I can't take care of them.
Maybe this is what
people think, are thinking
of me.
I could have done
more for myself.
I kinda got laid back.

Yeah, as far as that goes
I do. I blame myself.
But basically, I think
that it's his fault.

Camper in sister's backyard
Huntley, IL

Cari, (26) and Lisa: *She don't want to give up her kids*
Four children: Bobbi Ann 5, Toni Marie 4, Samantha Jo 3, Nicole Lee 19 months

When Cari talks it's in a whisper. Mostly Lisa, her sister, talks; and Cari listens with a detached expression as if she's listening to someone else's story.

Lisa has saved Cari and her four little girls from the shelters or worse the streets by letting them stay in her backyard camper—a white windowless box so cramped it's impossible to stand upright.

The two families are doubling up. And you can hear it, as well as see it, as Cari struggles to whisper her story to me, and Lisa prompts, and interrupts, and fills in the details. Their two voices are blending—doubling up. It's as if in losing her home, Cari has lost her voice, her own story, her sense of self. Or maybe it takes two women to tell this story.

CARI (LISA)

I.

Lisa: Cari couldn't stay with this man any longer. She didn't want to take the chance that he would abuse the kids.

Cari: He was an abuser.

Lisa: It took a lot of courage to leave him. But, it had to be his idea.

Cari: He found someone else.

Lisa: The only way she could get out of the situation.

Cari: The only way I could get away. He haunted me.

Lisa: He'd sit in his car. I had to get a bee bee gun. You come to my door and I'll fill you with bee bees.

Cari: He hunted me down when I tried to leave.

Lisa: He'd wait till my husband left and he'd show up at the door. Once he yanked her down the stairs by her hair right here in front of me.

Cari: It's fine with me that he has another woman.

Lisa: His idea because he's had enough.

II.

Cari: The best the county could do was to set me up in a motel—no cooking, no nothing.

Lisa: No way, we could never let them go to a motel with four children.

Cari: And then find my way back to Waukegan, to the soup kitchen.

Lisa: We couldn't let her do that. I mean four little girls sharing a bathroom with grown men.

Cari: But, I would have to do it.

Lisa: She gets no help from the father.

Cari: If I was alone, there would be no problem. Even with two kids.

Lisa: She don't want to give up her kids.

Cari: Just because I left an abusive man, I have to give up my kids. It just doesn't make any sense.

Lisa: I was afraid if they found out she had all these kids, they might consider taking them away from her. And that's why my husband said, "We can't let that happen."

III.

Cari: So, I've been living six weeks with my sister. My four kids and I sleep out in the camper. It sleeps six. We come inside during the day.

Lisa: Our major concern—What are we going to do with the winter coming? Where are we going to put the little kids?

Cari: Where are my four little girls going to sleep?

Lisa: Can't put them in one room, all six—counting my two kids.

Cari: Too cold to sleep out there.

Lisa: It does have heat.

Cari: I guess I have no other choice, unless I find a place. I'm worried that if someone finds out about me living in the back yard, they'll turn me in, or maybe they'll help find us a place.

Lisa: It's not that she's a bad mother. It's just that she has nowhere to stay. Is it fair to take away her kids because she has no roof over her head?

IV.

Lisa: I talked to this priest and he said there was this lady that could help her.

Cari: So I called.

Lisa: She said, "Have you talked to St. Francis?"
And Cari said, "No, who's he?"
She went, "He's a saint."
"You want me to talk to a saint?" Cari asked.

Cari: I thought it was some guy who was going to help me. I felt so stupid.
"Oh God, you expect me to talk to a saint?"
"You pray, and you'll find an answer."
And that was the only answer she had for me. Everyone else says wait.
But when you have four kids you just can't sit around and wait.

V.

Lisa: But the saddest thing is something Cari told me recently. She said, "With all the problems I've had, maybe I shouldn't have left. At least, I had a roof over my head."

Cari: If you leave a bad situation people say, "Oh, you had this." Like I should have stayed. They make me feel that if you leave an abuser, you're in the wrong. He has things. He's not hurting.

Lisa: He never kept a roof over their head even when they were together.

Cari: But it didn't seem so bad, because he would get money.

Lisa: Because he needed it.

Cari: People say to me, it's my fault. Why did you have four kids? I have them, so what do you want me to do with them? They're here. He insisted on a big family. He wanted a boy.

Lisa: And she gets no help from him.

Home of the Sparrow Interfaith Shelter
McHenry, IL
Donna *(27): I never call this a shelter*
Four children: Lee, Brent, Donald, Jimmy—all are under six years old

I sense hostility from Donna. How dare I invade her space, her shelter, her sanctuary.
Then once she begins her stories—-she relaxes with me and tells me how it is.

Donna may be without a home, but she carries around with her a sense of home that
four walls can't define. It's impossible to feel anything but bewilderment and empathy.
The low ceiling in the long, narrow Quonset house feels like it's touching my head.

DONNA

I.
I never call this a shelter
to them, my kids.
It's a house.
That's our bedroom.
I try to make it as normal as
possible. In the meantime I'm a
basket of nerves. But it beats the streets.
I came here because I knew
if we ever got caught
sleeping in the car
they'd take my kids. These kids
are my life. So here they're protected
too.

II.
My kids come first.
Brent takes it real hard. The first night
we were here he sat on the bed and said,
"I'm not staying
with all these people.
I want a house
of my own
I want my Dad.
Why isn't my Dad allowed
to come here?"

For a while Donald didn't know
his Dad. It broke his heart
because one day I handed Don
to him because Don always went
to bed by the time he visited.
He cried. It just killed him.

III.
When you come here you give up
every right as a human being
to have a roof over your head.
My husband is not allowed here
unless there's staff here.
I have to write a note for my kids
to spend the night at their grandmother's.
I try to be good but
these are my children and
someone is telling me how
to raise my kids
because I don't have
somewhere to live.
and it's really hard.
It's like living in hell.
I don't have
a choice to come here.
If I didn't, they would have taken Lee
because he had to go to school.

IV.
Just because we're homeless people and
can't find a place to live it's like you have no
say in anything. Saturday night I was blamed
for leaving my children—I was there.

I lost points for yelling.
You lose 4 points and
you're out of here.
There's no yelling or hitting
your children here.
Which makes it hard
for discipline sometimes:
4 points in a week
and you're out.
No matter what I say,
there's no proving you're innocence.
You're automatically guilty.
It's not like a court of law.

People across the street complained
I was yelling at my kids.
I was.
The bees were so bad.
There was a pear on the ground and
he dropped the blanket on the pear
which is covered with bees and
I'm yelling at him and
they think I'm yelling at the kids.

V.
But thank God we never slept in the car
we've never been that bad off.
But being in motels isn't a whole lot
better. People tell me
that being in other shelters is a lot worse
than this. But I don't know how
it could be worse.
My family is totally split up.

But thank God I have my kids.
Yesterday it got to the point
that I wanted to send them
to a foster home
to get out of here.
Because my word means nothing.
Because I live in a shelter
my rights are taken away from me.
I'm 27 years old.
I've had those 4 kids
always with me.
Because I'm homeless and
I can't find somewhere to live,
this is the result.
I don't know how much
longer I can take it.
This is the worse off
I've ever been.
It takes so little
to end up homeless.

St. Sylvester Shelter Home, Catholic Charities
Chicago, IL
Maria (37): *This isn't my fault*
Three children: Trina 14, Amanda 6, Matt 3

Maria is eight months pregnant with her fourth child. In the corner of the room against a wall, Matt, her three-year-old son, sits and plays with his shoes, which he's turned into two cars.

Like some fashion model Maria keeps toying with her blonde hair, moving it behind an ear, running her fingers through it. She's itchy for a cigarette. She brags that she smokes a pack a day. Her blue shirt stretches across her large belly and does nothing to hide her prominent breasts. Though there is a defiant tone to everything she says, she seems oblivious to her surroundings and circumstances.

MARIA

I.
Not presently married,
never been married.
They'll never see me.
They'll never know my last name.

Basically, I take care of myself.
My mother died when I was six.
My father doesn't want to be bothered.

II.
All my kids have different fathers.
Not that I play around,
because I don't.
They just look
at me and I get
pregnant. I almost thought
about an abortion with
this last baby. But I
couldn't do it. I just didn't
have the guts. That's not
my beliefs or whatever. He wanted
to pay for it, but he didn't want
to take me
down for the abortion. So
I kept the money and didn't
see him again. Why should I
even do it, if it's not what
I believe in? I didn't ask
for the money, he just
volunteered it. And I'm
going to keep the baby, too.

III.
Most of the time I tell them
I kept the better end
of the deal when they ask why
I had four kids. Besides
the situation might not have worked
out or they weren't ready
or they chickened out
or whatever. Sometimes
I look at it fine.
My kids are great
at times. They all have their bad
moments. That's what keeps me
going these kids. It's like
giving up whatever else.

IV.
I'm trying to tell you
in words. I don't know
what else to say.
This isn't my fault.
I'm just placing it
in my own words.
I don't feel
it's my fault.

ABOUT THE AUTHOR

Gail Lukasik was born in Cleveland, Ohio, and was a ballerina with the Cleveland Civic Ballet Company. Lisel Mueller described her book of poems, *Landscape Toward a Proper Silence*, as a "splendid collection." In 2002, she was awarded an Illinois Arts Council Award for her poem, "In Country."

She writes the Leigh Girard mystery series. *Kirkus Reviews* called her second Leigh Girard mystery, *Death's Door*, "fast-paced and literate, with a strong protagonist and a puzzle that keeps you guessing." Her debut stand-alone mystery, *The Lost Artist*, received praise from *Publishers Weekly* who said, "Rose's present-day sleuthing and the intertwined tale of the original homeowners command our interest until the final page."

She holds a Ph.D. in English and lives in Libertyville, Illinois with her husband.

Made in the USA
Monee, IL
10 April 2020